T0268668

THE WORLD
ACCORDING TO

Lee McQueen

Edited by Louise Rytter
Illustrations by Nabil Nezzar

Contents

A Kaleidoscopic Mind

Lee Alexander McQueen's contribution to fashion was revolutionary and his enduring legacy is still unmatched. He transformed fashion into ingenious poetry that left his audiences spellbound and broke down barriers with sensational shows that merged craftsmanship, heritage, technological innovation and imagination. McQueen was known for having over three hundred references in each of his collections and his kaleidoscopic mind was fuelled by a constant battle between lightness and darkness, life and death. His original ideas propelled 20th-century fashion into a new realm, and were turned into reality with the help of some of the most cutting-edge and skilled creatives working across photography, film, music, jewelry, millinery, makeup and footwear design. McQueen's work was autobiographical and he was deeply committed to it — as he said himself: 'My life is like an Edgar Allan Poe story: living for the love of one's life but sacrificing oneself for the love of work.'

He was born in 1969: the same year that Neil Armstrong took his first steps on the moon. The son of a taxi driver and a teacher, McQueen grew up drawing dresses on the walls of his bedroom in London's East End. Pursuing his dream of becoming a fashion designer, he left school at sixteen to train as a tailor's apprentice on Savile Row. After four years gaining experience at Anderson & Sheppard and Gieves & Hawkes, McQueen went on to work for the theatrical costumier Berman's & Nathan's, the Japanese designer Koji Tatsuno and Italian designer Romeo Gigli. Due to his extraordinary talent, he was given the opportunity to study at Central Saint Martins College of Art in London, and established his eponymous label after graduating from the MA Fashion course in 1992.

From 1996 to 2001, McQueen took on the additional role of Creative Director of Givenchy, translating his rebellious vision for a storied Parisian couture house. Joining the Gucci Group (now Kering) in 2001 offered McQueen an opportunity to expand the output of his own label, introducing menswear and fragrance as well as opening flagship stores across the world. Now established as a household name, McQueen was made Commander of the British Empire by the Queen for his services to fashion in 2003. In the same year he was also awarded International Designer of the Year by the Council of Fashion Designers of America, and named British Designer of the Year by the British Fashion Council four times throughout his career.

McQueen was a maverick storyteller with an idiosyncratic point of view. His catwalk shows now form part of fashion legend: from Kate Moss reincarnated as an ethereal hologram for 'The Widows of Culloden' (Autumn/Winter 2006) to Michelle Olley caged in a moth-filled asylum for 'Voss' (Spring/Summer 2001). McQueen's most iconic show moment was perhaps the finale of his 'No. 13' (Spring/Summer 1999) collection, which saw model Shalom Harlow being spray-painted by two robots in a dramatic spectacle inspired by the interaction between man and machine. His final fashion show 'Plato's Atlantis' (Spring/Summer 2010) also used robots to spark a dialogue — they moved down the catwalk alongside his models and filmed the audience. Streamed live on the internet to millions of people around the world — one of the first fashion shows to be presented as such — it put forward a prescient and powerful vision of the future. Yet again, McQueen had left his audience stunned.

At the time of McQueen's tragic death in 2010, fashion's biggest names paid tribute to his influence. American *Vogue* Editor-in-Chief Anna Wintour said of the designer: 'He brought a uniquely British sense of daring and aesthetic fearlessness to the global stage of fashion. In such a short career, Alexander McQueen's influence was astonishing — from street style, to music culture and the world's museums. His passing marks an insurmountable loss.' Milliner and close collaborator Philip Treacy called McQueen's talent 'supersonic'. Model Naomi Campbell, a friend of McQueen's, added that 'his talent had no boundaries, and he was an inspiration to everyone who worked with him and knew him'. His loss was also felt beyond the confines of the fashion industry. His legacy received the highest honour with the retrospective exhibition 'Alexander McQueen: Savage Beauty' at the Metropolitan Museum of Art (2011) and the Victoria & Albert Museum (2015), a blockbuster show visited by over one million people.

But who was Lee Alexander McQueen? How did London and his Scottish heritage inform his work? What was his view on women, and how did he define beauty and style? What fascinated him about tailoring and haute couture? What frustrated him about celebrity culture and the fashion industry? What inspired him and which artists influenced his work? How did nature and birds in flight intrigue him? What was the meaning behind his imaginative shows and sometimes controversial collections such as 'Highland Rape' (Autumn/Winter 1995)? Which show had the biggest emotional impact on him? This book offers an insight into the wit and wisdom of his genius by presenting over two hundred of his most honest, thought-provoking and humorous declarations. Selected from interviews spanning his two-decade career, the quotations track his evolution from working-class kid to international superstar.

McQueen was outspoken, radical and often misunderstood. The press described him as 'neurotic', a 'misogynist', an 'East End yob' and a 'bad boy'. He was in fact a sensitive, romantic and intelligent person who used his meticulous artistry and imagination to transform clothes, change attitudes and challenge the possibilities of fashion. He saw fashion as a weapon to empower women and a catalyst for questioning our perception of beauty. With courage and passion, McQueen created a new vision of the 'modern woman' by merging the energy of London, classic tailoring and haute couture with his own DNA, sense of innovation and masterful skill. There is no doubt that McQueen's absence from the world's fashion stage has left a huge void, but his unrivalled legacy will continue to intrigue and inspire generations to come.

Louise Rytter

Lee McQueen

on

Lee McQueen

I always knew
I would be
*SOMETHING IN
FASHION.*
I didn't know
how big,
but I always knew
I'd be
SOMETHING.

I was three years old when I started
drawing. I did it all my life. I always wanted
to be a designer. I read books on fashion from
the age of twelve. I followed designers' careers.
I knew Giorgio Armani was a window
dresser, Emanuel Ungaro was a tailor.

†

If you look under the wallpaper
at home, there's a picture of Cinderella
in a corset and bubble skirt that
I designed when I was three.

†

I am married to work.

What you see in the work
is the person himself.
And my heart is my work.

✝

Everything is personal to me.
I can't do anything that's not personal.
It has to be personal, otherwise I can't
see the point in doing it.

✝

You have to tell the difference between
the way that I talk and what I'm actually
saying. None of my companies has ever gone
bust, I employ fifty people, turnover
is massive. You don't get to do that by being
a twat, that takes an intelligent person.

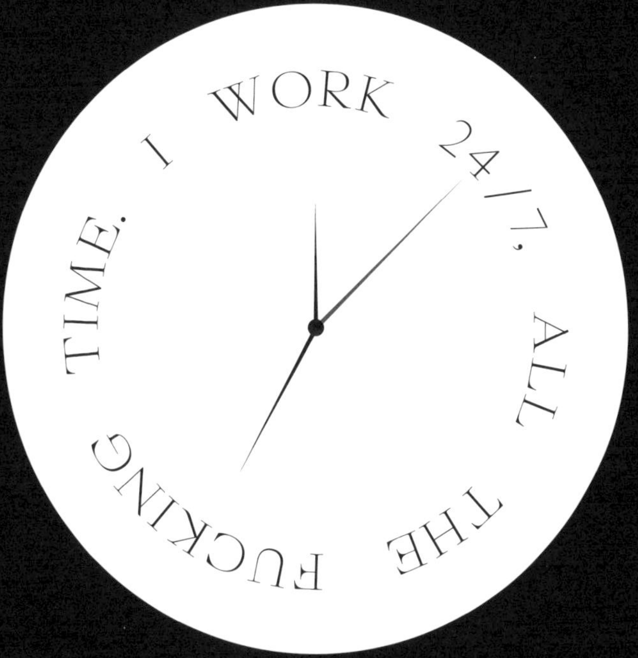
I WORK 24/7, ALL THE FUCKING TIME.

I seem to suffer from split personalities. I'm usually thinking or doing more than three jobs at the same time. It's the nature of the beast.

I'm a
working-class kid.

I stick to my
working-class

R O O T S

and that's what
gets me the press.

My collections have always been autobiographical, a lot to do with my own sexuality and coming to terms with the person I am — it was like exorcising my ghosts in the collections. They were to do with my childhood, the way I think about my life and the way I was brought up to think about life.

†

I'm a designer with a cause.
I like to challenge history.

†

People can take me as they find me.
Whatever else I've done, I've never tried
to be something I'm not.

Have a complete understanding that you're
good at [fashion] before trying. Otherwise
don't bother because it's not worth the pain.

†

I'm prepared to forget about money
if it affects my creativity because,
remember, I started off with nothing,
and I can do that again.

†

I'm never fazed by celebrity culture,
because whenever I get home, Dad will
always ask me to make him a cup of tea.

†

I can't get sucked into that celebrity
thing; I think it's just crass.

I ALWAYS
HAD THE
MENTALITY
THAT I ONLY
HAD ONE LIFE,
AND I WAS
GOING TO
DO WHAT
I WANTED
TO DO.

I know I'm

P
R
O
V
O
C
A
T
I
V
E.

You don't have to like it,

but you do have to
acknowledge it.

I came to terms with not fitting in
a long time ago. I never really fitted in.
I don't want to fit in.

†

Some of the most brilliant artists in the
world didn't talk posh and didn't fit in.
But a Van Gogh goes for £30m now.
It comes down to what's inside.

†

If I wasn't in fashion, I'd be in a
war zone being a photojournalist.

I want people to make mistakes
because something brilliant will evolve.
You have to break the codes.

†

I'm capable of doing anything as long
as it comes from the heart.

†

If people can't cope with a bit of honesty,
then that's their problem.

I LIKE TO

BREAK

DOWN

BARRIERS

I'm a romantic
schizophrenic.

Romance is where my heart is.

†

I don't think like the average person
on the street. I think quite
perversely sometimes.

†

I'm a big anarchist. I don't believe
in religion, or in another human being
wanting to govern over someone else.

†

People find my designs aggressive.
But I don't see them as aggressive.
I see them as romantic, dealing with
a dark side of personality.

I'm not an aggressive person, but I do
want to change attitudes. If that means
I shock people, that's their problem.

†

I've always had a fascination
with the macabre.

†

I oscillate between life and death,
happiness and sadness, good and evil.

You've just got
to have a bit of an

OPEN

MIND

not be so judgmental,
educate yourself in

THE WORLD OF ALEXANDER MCQUEEN.

2

Lee McQueen

on

Tailoring

I try   to push

          the silhouette.

To change   the silhouette

                    is to change

                    the thinking

          of how   we look.

Everything I do is based on tailoring.

†

I want to be the purveyor of a certain
silhouette or a way of cutting, so that
when I'm dead and gone people will know
that the 21st century was started
by Alexander McQueen.

†

It's always about pushing to the extreme:
the human body, human nature.

†

I like to think of myself as a plastic
surgeon with a knife.

I'm not talking in an elitist way but
everything that art's based around today has
no substance. There's no technique. And I
do believe that you should understand the
technique before you can destroy it.

†

The construction of Victorian clothes
was so tight and heavy and stiff.
I'm all for bringing back construction —
but making it modern and light.

†

I'm about construction
and manipulation.

I'm intent on chopping
things up.

Not chopping
them up to
destroy them,
chopping
them up to
distort them.

Fashion is like architecture — it's creative but technical, too.

A TAILORED JACKET
NARROWS INTO
THE WAIST.

THE

SHAPING
FOR MY SUITS
IS FITTED ON THE
CURVATURE OF THE SPINE.

I like things to be modern and still
have a bit of tradition.

†

I'm not one of these designers that
sit back and point to things. I can't work like
that. At the end of the day, I come from
the atelier myself. I come from Savile Row.

†

My designing is done mainly during
fittings. I change the cut.

I don't want to look at any shapes.
I don't want to reference anything: a picture,
a drawing. I want it all to be new.

†

As a designer you're always working
with cutting up the body to different
proportions, different shapes. This is
what a designer's job is, to transcend what
fashion is and what it could be.

I design from the side, that way I get the worst angle of the body. You've got all the lumps and bumps, the S-bend of the back, the bum. That way I get a cut and proportion and silhouette that works all the way round the body.

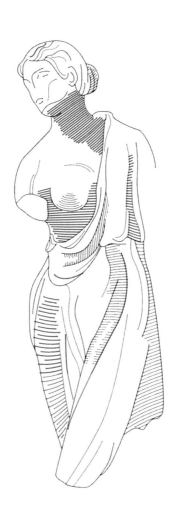

With bustles and nipped-
in waists, I was also
interested in the idea that
there are no constraints
on the silhouette. I wanted
to exaggerate a woman's
form, almost along the lines
of a classical statue.

There's nothing more *erotic* than a woman in a two-piece suit.

Through cutting, I try to draw attention
to our unrelenting desire for perfection.
The body parts that I focus on change
depending on the inspirations and
references for the collection and what
silhouettes they demand.

†

With the bumsters, it was an art thing,
to change the way women looked, just
by cut; to make a longer torso. But
I was taking it to an extreme. The girls
looked quite menacing because there was
so much top and so little bottom, because
of the length of the legs. That was the
concept, nothing to do with a 'builder's bum.'

That part of the body — not so much
the buttocks, but the bottom of the spine —
that's the most erotic part of anyone's
body — man or woman.

†

Tailoring is just a form of construction,
it's the rigour behind the design but,
at the end of the day, you're still dealing
with a single- or double-breasted jacket.
The narrative is what makes it interesting,
plus the romance behind it and the detail...
That's what makes McQueen
stand out: the detail.

I design clothes to flatter
real people, not models.
REAL PEOPLE
have lumps and bumps,
they have

('LOVE HANDLES')

AND I LIKE THAT.

My mates are
electricians, plumbers,
real workmen. I don't
like all that fluff, all that
camping it up.

3

Lee McQueen

on

Fashion

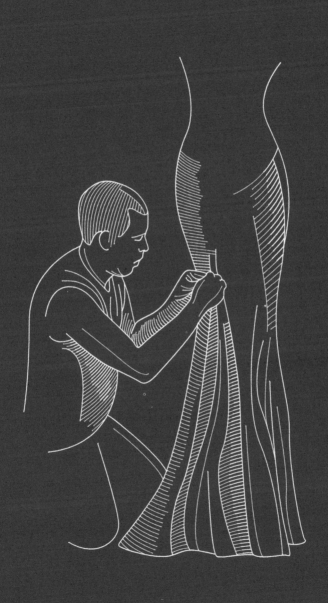

FASHION IS A BIG BUBBLE

AND
SOMETIMES
I FEEL LIKE
POPPING
IT.

If I were God, I would stop fashion
for five years. It needs to take time out.

†

Fashion is like any entertainment
industry — it's fickle.

†

Artistic expression is channelled through me.
Fashion is just the medium.

†

I never conformed to any sort
of fashion ideal. My idea was always
to show reality.

I wouldn't like to see my designs
on everyone — I'd go fucking mad.

†

You can't buy style.
Personal style is hard to come by.
Because you're born with it.

†

I don't think you can become a good
designer, or a great designer. To me,
you just are one. I think to know about
colour, proportion, shape, cut, balance
is part of a gene.

AS A DESIGNER,
YOU'VE ALWAYS
GOT TO PUSH YOURSELF
FORWARD
YOU'VE ALWAYS
GOT TO KEEP UP WITH
THE TRENDS

OR

MAKE

YOUR

OWN

TRENDS.

THAT'S WHAT I DO.

I especially like the accessory for its sadomasochistic aspect.

I believe the
sole purpose of
fashion is to

CREATE

and not

ACCUMULATE

I'm making points about the times
we live in. My work is a social document
about the world today.

†

I like to see aggression, not just for the
sake of being aggressive, but in the sense
of the way the design is attacked.

†

I like people to trace the future instead
of working with the norm. What's the
point of designing a mini skirt, if the
mini skirt is already there?

Fashion can be really racist, looking at the
clothes of other cultures as costumes ...
That's mundane and it's old hat.

†

What I am trying to bring to fashion
is a sort of originality.

†

My clothes give you an intensity
that you cannot bear. When something
makes you feel that deeply inside,
it makes you reflect on your own life.

It's what fashion is about — time to *experiment* and

push

boundaries.

Fashion should be
a form of escapism,
and not a form of

IMPRISONMENT

I wasn't born to
give you a

TWIN SET AND PEARLS

I can't see Anna Wintour
in a pair of bumsters.

†

I rely on my honesty and, in fashion,
it doesn't go down too well, because people
want to hear how good they are and
how nice their magazine is.

†

It's a constant chore to bring clothing
into the 21st century.

My clothes are seductive, they're very subversive, very dark. They leave a hidden mystery behind the person who's wearing them.

You should follow your heart, no matter
how difficult that feels. It's important
not to feel suffocated by the pressure
of becoming the next big fashion designer.

✝

I know what it's like to be a young
and struggling designer. It can be
demoralizing if you have a clear aesthetic
that's not immediately commercial
as other people don't get it.

✝

If I've influenced fashion,
it's by pissing everyone off.

I think I can say that
I have made my stamp on

LONDON
FASHION AND
INTERNATIONAL
FASHION

so I've done my job.

I want the
clothes to be

H   S
  E   M
    I   O
      R   O
        L

like they
used to be.

Ultimately, I do this to transform
mentalities more than the body. I try to
modify fashion like a scientist by offering
what is relevant to today and what will
continue to be so tomorrow.

†

I'm interested in designing for posterity.
People who buy McQueen are going
to hand the clothes down to their children
and that's very rare today.

4

Lee McQueen

on

Couture

Anything I do
is based on

craftsmanship.

Paris couture started with Charles Worth, who was English, and it will begin again with Alexander McQueen.

†

Couture is beyond beyond. It is where the dreams of your life in fashion become a reality.

†

Structure and finesse are what couture is all about. I don't want to embroider everything in sight or play around with loads and loads of tulle.

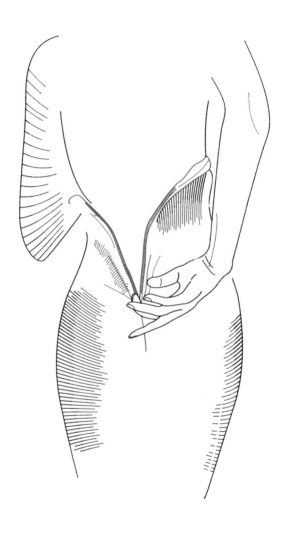

The clothes are not for
the 'modern woman',
but for the private woman
seeking to explore her own
mythical fantasies.

I think haute couture is for a select
few who can afford that sort of
workmanship. I think it should be quite
underground and personal.

†

Couture's not for the average person
on the street. I mean, you never see these
people. You never get invited to their dinner
parties. I just work for them.

†

People have to understand my background.
Before Central Saint Martin's I'd worked for
seven years in the business. I wasn't some
student who jumped into couture. The wives
of the customers I made suits for on Savile
Row are the women who buy couture.
I already knew that world.

HAUTE
COUTURE
IS AS
CLOSE
TO
ART

AS
FASHION
GETS.

Givenchy is based on a

CLASSIC,
CLEAN LINE

without the trend of the *now* or *never*.

Haute couture is about tradition,
and — coming from Savile Row —
I believe in tradition.

†

I'm not Givenchy,
I'm Alexander McQueen.

†

McQueen is about our times and
Givenchy is about allure — and it's fucking
hard to be both at the same time.

There's a certain way fashion should
go for a house of that stature,
not McQueen bumsters, I'm afraid.

†

When I did my first Givenchy couture
collection, I did not really understand
the way ahead for the house. Then I realized
the reason I am here is because of who
I am and what I do. But it became harder
because the workrooms could make every
dream I had a reality, and it is difficult
to know where to stop.

Givenchy is about the client.

McQUEEN IS ALL ABOUT ME.

The atelier and I, we have a universal language, even though I can't speak French. As soon as I start working with them, they know instantly when I start moving my hand.

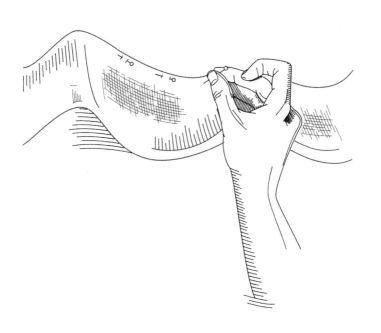

I think they really like me up there
in the atelier. They don't think I'm some
silly little kid from London fussing
around with a hemline.

✝

Working in the atelier was fundamental
to my career … Because I was a tailor,
I didn't totally understand softness, or
lightness. I learned lightness at Givenchy.
I learned to soften. For me, it was an
education. Working at Givenchy helped
me learn my craft.

I think that
couture
has complete
relevance today.

Designer fashion
shouldn't be

THROWAWAY

5

Lee McQueen

on

Fashion Shows

THE SHOW IS MEANT

TO PROVOKE

AN EMOTIONAL RESPONSE

IT'S MY 30 MINUTES TO DO

WHATEVER I WANT.

I need inspiration. I need something
to fuel my imagination and the shows
are what spur me on, make me excited
about what I'm doing.

†

I don't wanna do a cocktail party,
I'd rather people left my shows
and vomited. I prefer extreme reactions.

At the end of the day, I spend thirty grand on a show and have thirty minutes of six hundred people's attention. I think it's pointless doing a show that's not gonna say nothing, to be honest. If people are gonna leave your show without some sort of emotion, then I don't think you're doing a very good job.

†

I don't see any point in the audience leaving the show with no emotion. We're all human; we understand what turns us on and what turns us off. But you know it scares people to see what comes out when they're alone in their bedroom at night.

Storytelling is what we loved as kids, and this is what a show is about.

It motivates me to see an
illusion in my head and then
see the actual thing live.
It's a progression in my mind
and the evolution of what
I believe is fashion.

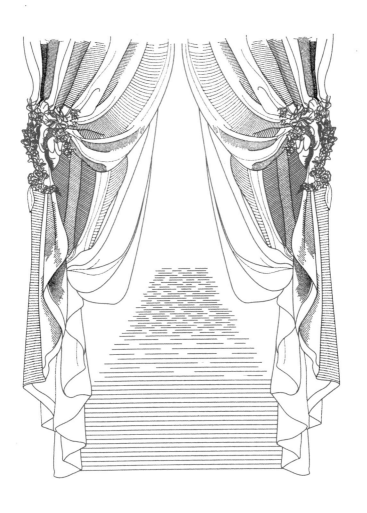

The shows
are about
what's

buried in
people's
psyches.

I use things that people want to hide
in their head. Things about war, religion,
sex, things that we all think about but don't
bring to the forefront. But I do and
I force them to watch it. And then they
start saying it's gross and I'm like:
'Actually love, you were already thinking
about all this, so don't lie to me'.

†

It's good to leave the audience
in bewilderment.

I used to do it to shock people,
to provoke a reaction, but now I just
do it for myself. The shows always reflect
where I am emotionally in my own life.

†

It was my best show, that moment with
Shalom ['No. 13', Spring/Summer 1999]!
That combination of arts and crafts
with technology — that weird unison
between man and machine.

The shows
are my own
living
nightmares.

Usually, the shows come
from a biographical place;
how I'm feeling at the time.
The audience is my therapist.
It's like an exorcism.

We broke
the mould by
not using the
fashion-show-
production
people.

There must always be some sort
of interaction with the audience to get
the message across that's going
through your mind.

†

I was never a big networker, but I was
a spin doctor — all those shock shows,
that's how I got my first backers.

†

I work with people who I admire and
respect. It's never because of who they are.
It's not about celebrity, that would show
a lack of respect for the work, for everyone
working on the shows.

With my shows, you do get the feeling —
the energy, buzz and excitement —
you'd get in a rock concert. I like blowing
people's minds. It's a buzz.

†

This is the birth of a new dawn in fashion.
There is no way back for me now.
I am going to take you on journeys you've
never dreamed were possible.

I DON'T NEED TO
HAVE *CELEBRITIES*
AT THE SHOW.

THE
CLOTHES

ARE THE
CELEBRITIES.

6

Lee McQueen

on

Great Britain

I like
London,

but

I love
Scotland

It's good to know where you come from.
It makes you what you are today.
It's DNA, it's in your blood.

†

My family were Celtics from the Isle
of Skye. I feel natural and at home
in Scotland more than England.

†

My mum traced the McQueen's back
to Skye and the Mull of Kintyre. I learned
about the Highland Clearances.

There's always an energy
in London: the poverty,
the unemployment, the drug-
induced environment, the
nightlife — it is the way
I predict my own clothes.
It is about the raw
energy of London.

I hate it when people romanticize
Scotland. There's nothing romantic about
its history. What the British did there
was nothing short of genocide.

†

'Highland Rape' [Autumn/Winter 1995]
was about England's rape of Scotland.

†

British fashion is self-confident and fearless.
It refuses to bow to commerce, thus
generating a constant flow of new ideas
while drawing on British heritage.

I still show
in London
because
I'm proud to
be a British
designer.

IT'S WHERE MY HEART IS AND WHERE I GET MY INSPIRATION

London's where I was brought up

We have such a multicultural society.
We have so much influence from around
the world all in one island. We are
always trendsetters. We don't follow,
we are creators.

†

When I received my CBE, the Queen
was so sweet. She smiled and her eyes
were so blue, and I just smiled back
and I felt like a duckling.

As a place for inspiration, Britain is the best in the world. You're inspired by the anarchy in the country.

Working on the suits for the Prince
of Wales, I used to sign the canvas
'McQueen was here' so I'd know I was
always close to his heart.

†

Britain always led the way in every field
possible in the world from art to pop music.
Even from the days of Henry VIII.
It's a nation where people come and gloat
at what we have as a valuable heritage,
be it some good, some bad, but there's
no place like it on Earth.

This is why
people come
to London.
They don't want
to see shift dresses
— they can go
anywhere in the
world to see that.

7

Lee McQueen

on

Women

Critics who labelled me

MISOGYNIST

got it all wrong.

When you see a woman wearing McQueen, there's a certain hardness to the clothes that makes her look powerful. It kind of fends people off. You have to have a lot of balls to talk to a woman wearing my clothes.

†

I grew up with three older sisters, and I saw them go through a lot of shit. I always wanted to be able to protect them. They would call me up to their room and I'd help them pick out clothes for work. Just, you know: 'what skirt with what cardigan?' But I was always trying to make them look strong and sheltered.

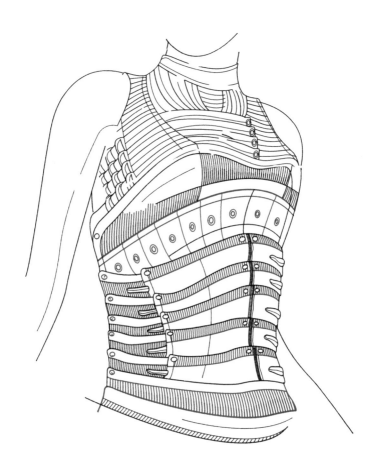

It's almost like putting
armour on a woman.
It's a very psychological
way of dressing.

I WANT PEOPLE TO BE *AFRAID* OF THE WOMEN I DRESS.

I design clothes because I don't want
women to look all innocent and naive,
because I know what can happen to them.
I want women to look stronger.

✝

There's always an underlying, sinister
side to women's sexuality in my work because
of the way I have seen women treated in my
life. Where I come from, a woman met a man,
had babies, moved to Dagenham, two-up two-
down, made the dinner, went to bed. That
was my image of women and I didn't want
that. I wanted to get that out of my head.

I don't like women to be taken advantage of.
I disagree with that most of all. I don't like
men whistling at women in the street,
I think they deserve more respect.

†

I don't see my clothes on a clothes
hanger. I'm trying to tap into
their lives, what will enhance them,
not myself or my ego.

†

I feel it's my job to give people that different
part of their personality — the opposite of
being demure — to hide behind.

I like men to
keep their distance
from women.

I like men to be
STUNNED
by an entrance.

I don't like frilly, fancy dresses.

Women can look beautiful and wear something well without looking fragile.

When I visualize a woman,
I visualize her mind and personality,
more than her physical self.

†

As times go along, I have grown to respect
women more. Especially as a gay man.
You don't come to touch on a physical
level. You get into their minds, about what
they need and what they would like.
And what they want to achieve. It's like
being a surgeon of the mind.

†

It's not like you see a beautiful woman
and she becomes your muse. It's more
in the minds of the women in the past,
like Catherine the Great, or Marie Antoinette.
People who were doomed. Joan of Arc
or Colette. Iconic women.

If you look at all their personalities
[Isabella Blow, Daphne Guinness,
Maiko Rothermere, Annabelle Neilson,
Plum Sykes — McQueen's muses], the world
they live in, they are all out on a limb.
They're not refined like the woman in a
John Singer Sargent. They're like punks
in their own world.

†

Isabella [Blow] flew. Her way of thinking
brought light into fashion. Even when
she was down, she was up with what
she wore. I had the best times with Isabella.
I remember going to Mauritius with her
and I'd come back from scuba diving and
it would be one hundred degrees and she'd
be standing on the beach head-to-toe in
McQueen with a Philip Treacy hat on.

TIPPI HEDREN PUSHED TO THE MAX...

She's the McQueen woman, isn't she?

8

Lee McQueen

on

Inspiration

Inspiration doesn't come with a notepad... it's eclectic. It comes from Degas and Monet and my *sister-in-law in Dagenham*.

In any collection, there are probably
over three hundred concepts I'm referencing.

✝

Influences are from my own imagination
and not many come from direct sources.
They usually come from, say, the way
I want people to perform sex or the way
I want to see people act. It's from a big
subconscious or the perverse.

I get blocked all the time, but I work
best under pressure. I can design
a collection in a day and I always do.

†

It's not a specific way of thinking, it's just
what's in my mind at the time. It could be
anything: it could be a man walking down the
street or a nuclear bomb going off. It could
be anything that triggers some sort of emotion
in my mind. I mean, I see everything in
a world of art in one way or another.
How people do things. The way people kiss.

I GET MY
IDEAS
OUT OF MY
DREAMS.

My mind has to be
completely focused on
my own illusions.

I draw inspiration from
the streets of the city:

from the
KIDS IN HOXTON,

to the
PUNKS IN CAMDEN,

to a

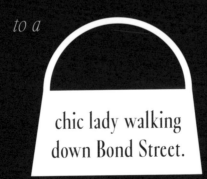

chic lady walking
down Bond Street.

†

The inspiration behind the hair used
as a label came from Victorian times when
prostitutes would sell theirs for kits of hair
locks, which were bought by people to give
to their lovers. I used it as my signature label
with locks of hair in Perspex. In the early
collections, it was my own hair: it was about
me giving myself to the collection.

I gather some influence from the Marquis
de Sade because I actually think of him
as a great philosopher and a man of his time.
Where people found him a pervert, I find
him influential in the way he provokes
people's thoughts. It kind of scares me.

†

I also love the macabre thing you see
in Tudor and Jacobean portraiture.

My favourite
art is Flemish.
Memling and
Van Eyck.
The Arnolfini
Marriage is one
of my favourite
paintings.

People keep on asking me:
do I ever run out of ideas?
How do you better that show,
and how do you better the
chess match ['It's Only a
Game', Spring/Summer 2005]?
Or how do you better the
snow show ['The Overlook',
Autumn/Winter 1999]? I don't
know where it comes from.
There is someone up there
saying 'do this one now'.

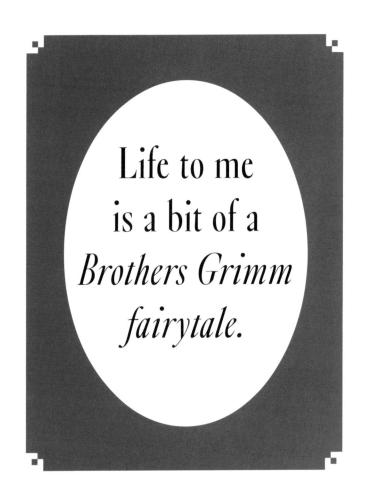

Life to me
is a bit of a
Brothers Grimm
fairytale.

I first saw this painting [*The Execution of Lady Jane Grey* by Paul Delaroche] fifteen years ago. Being a hopeless romantic, the emotion evoked that day has never left me.

†

I am always on the National Geographic and History channels. I am a sucker for history. I draw on it all the time.

†

I got the idea for the Armadillo shoes from H. R. Giger, and seeing *Alien*, and then I got a sculptor to make up a shoe so that it looked like it grew right out of the foot. Sick, ain't I?

†

I typed 'Atlantis' into Wikipedia,
and the first thing that came up was Plato's
definition of it and where he thought it was.
Atlantis is a metaphor for me of Neverland.
It could be anywhere in your mind.
Anywhere people find sanctuary in bad
times. As far as we know it didn't exist.
But if it did, it's a place I'll visit myself.

WHEN
TIMES
ARE HARD,
FANTASY
AND
ESCAPISM
ARE
CRUCIAL.

9

Lee McQueen

on

Nature

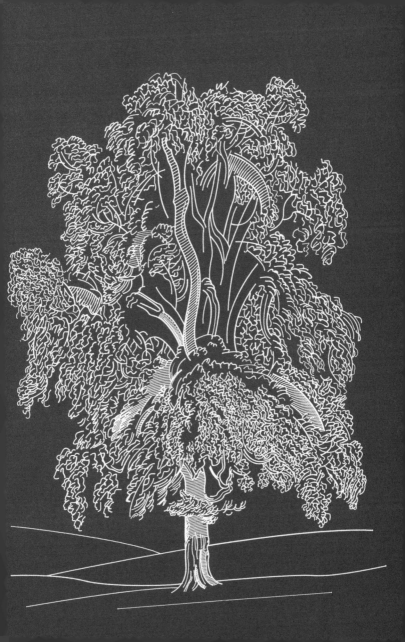

EVERYTHING
I DO IS
CONNECTED
TO

IN
ONE
WAY OR
ANOTHER.

I've done loads of collections based
on man and machine and man and nature,
but ultimately my work is always in some
way directed by nature. It needs to connect
with the Earth. Things that are processed
and reprocessed lose their substance.

†

Nothing will ever be more
beautiful than nature.

Birds in flight fascinate me.
I admire eagles and falcons.
I'm inspired by a feather
but also its colour, its
graphics, its weightlessness
and its engineering. It's so
elaborate. In fact, I try and
transpose the beauty
of a bird to women.

The whole show's feeling was about the Thompson's gazelle ['It's a Jungle Out There', Autumn/Winter 1997]. It's got these dark eyes, the white and black with the tan markings on the side, the horns — but it is the food chain of Africa. As soon as it's born it's dead, I mean you're lucky if it lasts a few months … and that's how I see human life, in the same way. We can all be discarded quite easily … you're there, you're gone, it's a jungle out there!

†

I was interested in the Industrial Revolution because, to me, that was when the balance shifted, man became more powerful than nature, and the damage really started.

Nature
is a
fabric
itself.

Animals fascinate me
because you can find
a force, an energy, a fear
that also exists in sex.

I feel most
at peace
under water.

We're in danger of killing the planet
through greed. Every species is fragile,
but animals are the underdogs while
we are actually bringing about our own
extinction — and theirs.

†

The shells had outlived their usefulness
on the beach, so we put them to another use
on a dress. During the show ['Voss', Spring/
Summer 2001] Erin O'Connor came out and
trashed the dress, so their usefulness was over
once again. Kind of like fashion, really.

†

I have an affinity with the sea,
maybe it's because I'm a Pisces.
It's very calming.

10

Lee McQueen

on

Beauty

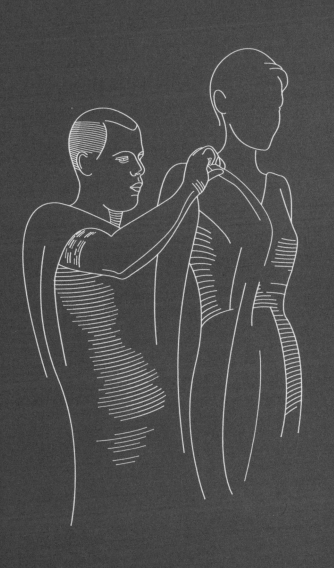

Life isn't perfect
and we're
not all perfect.

We are not all
size zero models.

THERE
IS BEAUTY
WITHIN.

I think there is beauty in everything.
What 'normal' people would
perceive as ugly, I can usually see
something of beauty in it.

†

From heaven to hell and back again,
life is a funny thing. Beauty can come
from the strangest of places, even the
most disgusting of places.

It's the ugly things
I notice more, because
other people tend to ignore
the ugly things.

LEE McQUEEN ON BEAUTY

You look at all the mainstream magazines
and it's all about the beautiful people,
all of the time. I wouldn't swap the team
I've been working with for a supermodel.
They've got so much dignity and there's
not a lot of dignity in high fashion. I think
they're all really beautiful.

†

There's beauty in anger. Anger for me
is a passion. If you don't have passion for
something, you shouldn't be doing it in the
first place. How can you move something
forward, if you are not confrontational? There
comes a point where you just have to block
off commercialism and do it from the heart.

BEING RADICAL
IS ABOUT
CHALLENGING
WHAT'S
ACCEPTED AND
WHAT'S NOT.
SOMETIMES IT'S

VULGAR,

BUT BEAUTY
COMES OUT
OF THAT.

I find beauty
in the grotesque,
like most artists.

I have to force
people to look
at things.

There's something … kind of
Edgar Allan Poe, kind of deep and kind
of melancholic about my collections.

†

I find beauty in melancholy.

†

People ignore the ugly things in life,
but within this they are missing the beauty
that lies under the rotten fruit.

With me, metamorphosis
is a bit like plastic surgery,
but less drastic.

Remember Sam Taylor-Wood's dying fruit?
Things rot ... I used flowers [in 'Sarabande',
Spring/Summer 2007] because they die.
My mood was darkly romantic at the time.

†

I appreciate Joel-Peter Witkin's work
with the same depth of feeling as that
of Bosch. The photograph 'Leda and the
Swan' is one of my favourite pieces.
I find the man so graceful.

†

It is important to look at death because
it is a part of life. It is a sad thing: melancholy
but romantic at the same time. It is the
end of a cycle — everything has to end.
The cycle of life is positive because it gives
room for new things.

It's not so
much about
death,

but the
awareness
that it is
there.

Sources

BOOKS

Andrew Bolton, *Alexander McQueen: Savage Beauty*, New York: Metropolitan Museum of Art, 2011 · Chloe Fox, *Vogue on: Alexander McQueen*, Quadrille Publishing Ltd, 2012l · Claire Wilcox ed., *Alexander McQueen*, London: Harry N. Abrams, Victoria & Albert Museum, 2015

MAGAZINES, NEWSPAPERS AND WEBSITES

AAP Newsfeed · AnOther · AnOtherMan · Art Review · British Vogue · Dazed & Confused · Domus · Drapers · Elle US · Harper's Bazaar · Harpers & Queen · Index · i-D · Interview · L'Officiel · Muse · Numéro · Nylon · Purple · Reuters · Self Service · SHOWstudio · Sky · Style.com · Tatler · Time Out (London) · The Cut · The Daily Mirror · The Daily Telegraph · The Evening Standard · The Face · The Fashion · The Financial Times · The Gazette · The Guardian · The Independent · The International Herald Tribune · The Metropolitan Museum of Art (metmuseum.org) · The New Yorker · The New York Times · The Pink Paper · The Scotsman · The Sunday Times · The Times · The Victoria & Albert Museum (vam.ac.uk) · American Vogue · W · Women's Wear Daily · Wynn

DOCUMENTARIES

'Breaking the Rules – Fashion Rebel Look', *British Style Genius* (BBC Two, 2008) · 'Cutting Up Rough', *The Works* (BBC Two, 20 July 1997) 'A Chat with Alexander McQueen' (Fashion Television) 'Fashion in Motion: Alexander McQueen' (Victoria & Albert Museum, June 1999)

MISC

Show notes, 'Natural Dis-tinction Un-Natural Selection' (Alexander McQueen, Spring/Summer 2009)

About the Author

Louise Rytter is a freelance fashion curator, strategist and online editor. Formerly Assistant Curator at the Victoria & Albert Museum, she worked on the blockbuster exhibition 'Alexander McQueen: Savage Beauty'. She was Content Editor on the world's largest virtual exhibition of style 'We Wear Culture' at Google Arts & Culture. She is the co-author of *Louis Vuitton Catwalk: The Complete Fashion Collections* (2018), also published by Thames & Hudson.

First published in the United Kingdom in 2022 by
Thames & Hudson Ltd, 181A High Holborn, London WC1V 7QX

First published in the United States of America in 2022 by
Thames & Hudson Inc., 500 Fifth Avenue, New York, New York 10110

The World According to Lee McQueen © 2022
Thames & Hudson Ltd, London

Foreword and edited compilation © 2022 Louise Rytter

Illustrations © 2022 Nabil Nezzar

Designed by Hannah Montague

British Library Cataloguing-in-Publication Data
A catalogue record for this book is available from the British Library

Library of Congress Control Number 2021934177

ISBN   978-0-500-02415-7

Printed and bound in China by C & C Offset Printing Co. Ltd

MIX
Paper from
responsible sources
FSC® C008047
FSC
www.fsc.org

Be the first to know about our new releases,
exclusive content and author events by visiting
thamesandhudson.com
thamesandhudsonusa.com
thamesandhudson.com.au